Original title:

Fiddle-Leaf Reflections

Author: Harrison Blake

ISBN HARDBACK: 978-1-80581-769-7
ISBN PAPERBACK: 978-1-80581-296-8
ISBN EBOOK: 978-1-80581-769-7

Fronds and Memories

In corners wide, they sway and dance,
Dust bunnies watch, they take a chance.
Cat thinks it's a jungle gym, oh dear,
Leaves whisper secrets, loud and clear.

Water in hand, I trip and spill,
Plant grows more, it gets a thrill.
Light shines in, the dust just beams,
My leafy friend knows all my dreams.

The Green Hour's Serenade

When evening falls, the shadows creep,
My plant begins to take a leap.
Chasing light with leafy flair,
Waves goodbye to the sun, with care.

I serenade my palm with cheer,
It blinks back, as if to hear.
A metaphorical fiddle, I pluck,
This indoor grove, well, what the luck!

Dreaming in Leafy Hues

Dreams of green in the sunny glow,
My house is now a leafy show.
Friends come around, they gasp and stare,
"Is it a plant or a circus fair?"

Photosynthesis on toast, we munch,
Conversations bloom, in a haphazard bunch.
Tell me your woes, dear leaf, I plead,
It nods politely, my leafy steed.

Silence of the Indoor Grove

In quietude, the leaves conspire,
A fancy world, they never tire.
Whispers floating, a gentle tease,
Imagination dances with ease.

The spider spins tales of woe,
While me and my plant, put on a show.
In this space, we take a bow,
To nature's humor, oh so wow!

Memories Beneath the Canopy

Beneath oversized leaves,
I spy ants on their quest,
With nature's green circus,
It beats all the rest.

They march in a line,
With snacks far too grand,
Carrying crumbs from lunch,
An unlikely band.

The sun peeks through gaps,
Like a game of hide and seek,
And the wind starts to sing,
In a whispering cheek.

A chameleon glances,
At his leafy attire,
With clothes so absurd,
Does he think he's on fire?

Dance of the Emerald Leaves

The leaves swirl around,
In a tango so bright,
They sway to the rhythm,
Of day turning night.

A squirrel joins in,
With moves quite absurd,
Spinning and flipping,
He jumps like a bird.

Each leaf's a dancer,
With steps of their own,
Twisting and twirling,
In green leafy tone.

When the breeze kicks up,
It's a grand masquerade,
With nature as the stage,
And fun never fades.

Echoes in a Pot

In a pot on my table,
An echo of green hears,
A whisper of sunshine,
And giggles of tears.

With soil as their blanket,
Roots stretch for the sky,
They chuckle at shadows,
As they wave bye-bye.

Each drop of water, a joke,
Splashing joy all around,
They laugh at my gardening,
With roots underground.

And when night falls down,
They hold secret chats,
About the silly dreams,
Of squirrels and spats.

Serpentines of Sunlight

Sunbeams sneak through leaves,
Like playful little sprites,
They bounce off the walls,
In marvelous flights.

Each ray is a dancer,
With moves that entice,
Tickling the spirits,
Of plants that are nice.

As shadows jump and play,
Underneath the tree's dome,
The sunlight plays tag,
With the greenery's home.

And if you look closely,
You'll see laughter unfold,
In the twists and the turns,
Of the sun's shining gold.

Boughs of Identity and Home

In the corner, I stand tall,
With leaves sprawling, a leafy wall.
I soak up sun like a lazy cat,
What should I wear? A coat or a hat?

Neighbors gossip, they peek and pry,
"That plant thinks it’s a stand-up guy!"
I sway and bend, a little too proud,
But really, I’m just a leaf in the crowd.

Mapping the Leafy Trails

With every leaf, I chart a quest,
A leafy map, I've got the zest!
Winding paths of whimsical greens,
Follow me to the land of dreams!

My leaves shout, "Look at me glide!"
On breezy days, I take such pride.
But when the cat leaps, oh dear me,
I’m just a plant, not a trapeze MC!

The Ethereal Dance of Green

Shaking my leaves to some funky beats,
A potted dancer with hidden feats.
Twisting and turning in sunlight's sway,
Modeling the newest leaf ballet!

A sprinkle of dust? Oh what a sight!
Dancing with shadows in the evening light.
But when I trip, a clumsy plant,
I blame the cat for my wild flant!

Chasing Meteor Showers Among Leaves

Tonight, I chase those twinkling lights,
With leaves like arms sharing my delights.
Each star that falls is a playful tease,
I reach up high, oh what a breeze!

I giggle as I sway and bend,
In my leafy world, there's no end.
But when it rains, oh what a fuss,
I'll stay inside, in my plant bus!

Harmony of Flora and Home

In the corner, a plant does sway,
It steals the sunshine, day by day.
Pantry's full, yet still I feed,
My leafy friend with utmost need.

It's hard to know just what they think,
Some days they water, others they stink.
Watch them dance when there's a breeze,
They move like they've got their own expertise.

With pots and soils, a messy floor,
I trip on leaves, oh what a chore!
Yet every time, I laugh and sway,
For green companions are here to stay.

The Secret Life of Houseplants

At midnight hour, they start to plot,
Chasing shadows, what a lot!
In the moonlight, they have a ball,
Swinging leaves like a plant brawl.

With tiny hearts, they whisper low,
Plotting schemes with the kitchen dough.
I swear I caught them in a toast,
Toasting to me, their clueless host!

Sometimes they look like they're about to burst,
Sharing gossip is their thirst.
Oh, to be a fly on that wall,
Hearing secrets in their leafy hall.

Echoes of Wilderness Indoors

In this jungle, slightly bizarre,
Plants move in like they own the bar.
Vines creep closer, they want a drink,
“Not so fast,” I say, “I need to think!”

Cacti laugh while succulents tease,
In this room, I bow to their ease.
They curl and twist, without a care,
Wishing for shoes, they’d love to wear.

A pet snake stares, it’s quite absurd,
Do plants pretend to be disturbed?
I catch them leafing through my books,
Learning to dance with all their hooks.

A Dance of Leaves and Threads

Leaves pirouette in sunny spaces,
Waving at me in leafy graces.
Threads of vines in grand ballet,
Twisting around in a stylish way.

My house feels like a green café,
With plants that laugh, 'Come on, let's play!'
A pothos did the cha-cha slide,
While I just watched with eyes wide.

They plot their routes on window sills,
Dreaming of mountains, blissful thrills.
I sprinkle jokes and watch them sway,
In our dance, they steal the day!

Daydreams Cradled in Green

In a pot of dreams, I sprout,
With leaves that giggle, there's no doubt.
Sunlight tickles, shadows dance,
In my leafy realm, there's a chance.

Sipping rain from silver cups,
Dodging bugs and their little hiccups.
A gentle breeze, I wave hello,
Wishing for a garden party show.

Dancing roots beneath my skin,
Whispers of mischief, where to begin?
Twisting vines with a graceful trend,
A chatty plant, it's hard to pretend.

A squirrel stops, stares at me,
"Are you a tree or just carefree?"
I chuckle deep, "Oh can't you see?
I'm the life of the party, just let me be!"

The Invisible Thread of Nature

In greenery, laughter spins and sways,
Chatty leaves sharing their funny ways.
Plant puns flying through the air,
With each rustle, they tend to share.

A worm nudges, “What’s in a leaf?”
“More jokes and wisdom — it’s beyond belief!”
Sunlight winks, casting a grin,
Nature’s humor, where do I begin?

Chasing shadows, the petals prance,
Holding a leaf in a silly dance.
The trees giggle in wind’s soft embrace,
Whispering secrets at a cozy pace.

A bumblebee buzzes a goofy song,
While flowers sway, they all sing along.
In this tapestry of green so bright,
The invisible thread ties laughter tight!

Lush Reflections In Still Water

In quiet pools where the lilies float,
I spy my reflection, can you take a gloat?
A leaf like a hat, a wink in my eye,
“Who’s the fairest?” I ask the sky.

Fishy friends swim by, all aglow,
“Meditate, my friend, let your worries go!”
I splash with joy, making ripples wide,
Creating giggles I can't hide.

Dragonflies buzzing, a flash of cheer,
“Join me in laughter, let’s have no fear!”
They swirl around, in a jig so sweet,
Nature’s dance, with a rhythmic beat.

As night falls, the stars turn bright,
Reflecting my silliness, pure delight.
In water's embrace, I play and twirl,
In this leafy world, I’m the silly pearl!

Sheltered in Leafy Embrace

Under the canopy where the laughter grows,
I find my refuge, as the humor flows.
The leaves shimmy, teasing the breeze,
In this leafy haven, I'm always at ease.

Hiding from shadows, tickled by sun,
Each petal a giggle, oh what fun!
Squirrels gossip, sharing their finds,
Stories of acorns and tangled vines.

The chubby caterpillar spins a tale,
Of a leafy ball where the bugs set sail.
With a chuckle, I join in the cheer,
For every whisper, nature holds dear.

Resting beneath this emerald dome,
I chuckle softly, feeling at home.
In a leafy embrace, I dance with glee,
For the funny side of life is always free!

Whispers of An Indoor Sanctuary

In corners bright where green things dwell,
A leafy friend, who knows me well.
With broad green arms, it stretches wide,
And sometimes keeps my secrets inside.

It dances lightly in the breeze,
A leafy diva, if you please!
I swear it rolls its eyes at me,
As I talk to it like therapy.

When sunlight hits, it gives a glow,
I think it laughs at my bad show.
A sprightly giggle in the air,
Is it a plant? Or is it flair?

In our small room, it's quite the star,
With me, it's traveled near and far.
Together, we create a scene,
A comical duo, evergreen!

The Spirit of Growth and Grace

Oh, how you grow from little seed,
With absurd ideas, oh yes indeed!
You spread your limbs like a dance in space,
With grace so fine, I can't keep pace.

I water you daily, don't want you to pout,
Yet you seem to grow when I'm out!
You perk up each time I leave the room,
Making sure I return to your bloom.

You strut your stuff in the sun's embrace,
Do I see a wink on that leaf's face?
It's like you're saying, "Watch me thrive!"
With each new leaf, I jump, I jive!

In our indoor jungle, what a show,
With plants like you, I'll never be low.
You keep it funny, you keep it bright,
My quirky friend, my leafy delight!

Roots of Serenity in Manmade Sanctuaries

In pots of green, they twist and sway,
With soil that dreams of yesterday.
They soak up sun like it's a treat,
In plastic homes, they kick their feet.

The neighbors laugh at leaves that dance,
While I give my plants a loving glance.
With every poke and every leaf,
They thrive on joy, not just belief.

In crowded rooms, they stand so tall,
Pretending they're at a garden ball.
They whisper secrets to the air,
While I sit back without a care.

Oh, roots of peace in pots so round,
You make my day without a sound.
With you, dear leaves, I find my bliss,
And smile at life in all its twists.

The Language of Leaves in Silence

Leaves chatter softly, no need for words,
Telling tales of dancing birds.
They wiggle-waggle like they're fun,
In bright green dresses, one by one.

The branches stretch like lazy arms,
As if to beckon all the charms.
Each leaf a story, each leaf a song,
Whispers of joy where they belong.

In the stillness, they laugh and play,
Breezy giggles in a sunlit bay.
They poke their heads over the rim,
And giggle softly, on a whim.

Oh, how they flutter, bringing cheer,
With messages we all hold dear.
In stillness found, they share their woes,
A language known, just through their prose.

Whispers of the Green Veins

Green veins talk, oh what a show,
In silent chats that ebb and flow.
With every breeze, their secrets spill,
A leafy gossip, a nature thrill.

They point and poke at busy feet,
While sipping sun and feeling sweet.
In look of wonder, they do inspire,
As I plant dreams to reach much higher.

Branches wave and do a jig,
In the comfort of the big and big.
They tease the air with leafy flair,
While I sit and just stop to stare.

Oh, whispering bones of vibrant green,
In their fun world, I can't be mean.
Together, we plot a fun escape,
From the busy hum of the urban drape.

In the Shadow of Living Light

In sunlit spots where shadows play,
The plants do party every day.
They stretch and yawn, and then they giggle,
In radiant rays, they dance and wiggle.

Underneath the lamp's warm glow,
They cast wild forms, a joyful show.
By moonlight's grace, they start to scheme,
In leafy dreams where they gleam.

Tickled by the morning sun,
They whisper secrets, just for fun.
In living shades, with moves so light,
They turn my worries into bright.

Oh, under lights, we all take flight,
In this crazy, leafy delight.
Together we laugh, we twist and sway,
In shadows of joy, we find our way.

Luminous Leaves in a Sunlit Corner

In the corner where sunlight plays,
Leaves giggle in whimsical ways.
A twist, a turn, a leafy sway,
They bask in warm, golden rays.

Sticky fingers on glassy panes,
They poke their heads, ignoring rains.
Conversations with dust motes fly,
Who knew leaves could be so spry?

When shadows stretch and night draws near,
They whisper jokes we cannot hear.
With each rustle, a cheeky tease,
“Who needs a tree when you have these?”

So, let them dance, those luminous greens,
With every chuckle, life redeems.
In a sunny nook where laughter’s rife,
Leaves inhabit a giggling life.

Whispers of Green in Urban Spaces

Among the concrete, they digress,
Those leaves of green, a verdant mess.
Peeking from windows with cheeky flair,
“Please send us sunlight and fresh air!”

In traffic jams, they shake their heads,
“Why are you stuck? Go home to beds!”
They gossip about passerby frowns,
With leaf-like smiles, they wear no crowns.

At cafés where humans sip their lattes,
They sense the blues that life berates.
“Join in our green party, don’t you know?
We make better friends than this quick flow!”

As puddles splash with careless glee,
They cheer, “Let’s dance!” with a rustling spree.
In every nook, they’re here to stay,
Whispers of green, brightening our day.

Beneath the Canopy of Dreams

In the midst of dreams, where shadows weave,
Leaves tell stories that make you believe.
Underneath, they chuckle and sigh,
Dreaming of clouds and a starry sky.

Twinkling lights through branches tease,
"Don't be shy, just lounge with ease."
Under their cover, the winks abound,
As sleepy thoughts skip all around.

As night descends, they link their arms,
"Who needs sleep? We've got charms!"
They plot and plan for the day ahead,
"Let's throw a bash before we're fed!"

So, nestle close to that leafy dome,
Where dreams take flight and laughter roams.
In their embrace, feel light and free,
A canopy of joy, just you and me.

Leaves that Dance with Shadows

In the twilight, shadows play,
Leaves boogie like it’s their day.
They shimmy with each passing breeze,
Teasing night with cheeky ease.

“Catch me if you can” they sway,
As flickering lights join the fray.
With every twist, the world's aglow,
Dancing leaves steal every show.

Moonlight’s laughter tricks the eye,
“Leap!” they cry and oh, they fly!
Spinning tales in their leafy choir,
Waltzing on with glee and fire.

So join the frolic, the sprightly cheer,
Dance along, for all’s sincere.
In the night where shadows prance,
Leaves have mastered the art of dance!

A Medley of Leaf and Light

In the corner blooms a giant leaf,
With a flair, it stirs up some grief.
It whispers to the cat with glee,
"Try to catch me, if you please!"

Sunlight dapples its broad expanse,
Daring shadows to join the dance.
The dog looks puzzled, with a frown,
As the plant sways, wearing its crown.

A little bug hops on for fun,
"What a ride! Oh, isn't this a pun?"
The leaf laughs, a hearty chuckle,
"Stay awhile, don’t burst my bubble!"

As evening sets and lights are dim,
The antics of the plant grow grim.
"Enough games, it's time for sleep!"
And in the dark, they start to leap.

Echoing Green in Still Life

In a pot of green, a leaf takes flight,
Spreading tales of the day and night.
"Look at me, the star of this show!"
Said the leaf, dancing to and fro.

Outside the window, winds do tease,
Swirling whispers among the trees.
"Don't you dare compare me to grass!"
The leaf exclaimed, full of sass.

Each raindrop falls, a playful cue,
Rolling off in a sparkling hue.
The leaf giggles, in high delight,
"I'm not your average plant in sight!"

But when the sun begins to fade,
The laughter dims, a masquerade.
"Time to rest, my leafy friend,
Tomorrow's fun will never end!"

Reverberations of Indoor Flora

In a cozy room, plants congregate,
Telling tales of their leafy fate.
"Last week, I swayed like a pro!"
Said the sprout with an ego to grow.

A creeping vine joins in the chat,
"Once I tangled a curious cat!"
Laughter erupts as they recall,
Their indoor mischief, one and all.

The succulent rolls its tiny eyes,
"You think you're clever with your lies?"
They banter on through every leaf,
A comedy show beyond belief!

As the moon glows high in the night,
The plants settle in, dimming their light.
"Goodnight, friends, till we meet anew,
For more antics, just us few!"

The Language of Leafy Breath

Oh, how the leaves exchange wise cracks,
In their green world, no one keeps tracks.
A bold phloem starts the jest,
"I’m the best, forget the rest!"

Petals giggle, swaying with flair,
While the stamen broadcasts the air.
"Can you hear me? I'm quite the charmer!"
Leafy banter, brought with armor.

A whisper floats through the room so bright,
"We’re the stars of this indoor sight!"
And with each breeze that passes near,
They laugh and dance, shedding no fear.

But as silence creeps and darkness arrives,
They hush their tales, where humor thrives.
"Goodnight, dear friends, in our leafy bed,
Tomorrow's laughter, like stars, we’ll spread!"

The Heartbeat of Leafy Companions

In the corner sits a potted friend,
With leaves so big, they never bend.
Telling secrets in the room's soft light,
They gossip nightly, what a sight!

I watered them once, they looked quite bold,
Now they dance like they're made of gold.
But I swear that plant learns all my quirks,
It winks at me when I do my jerks!

When I make coffee, they catch the heat,
Their leafy arms wiggle to the beat.
I swear I heard a leaf say, "Who's next?"
I chuckled aloud, feeling quite vexed!

Who knew these greens could crack a grin?
With plant humor, I'm destined to win.
A leafy companion with a heart so true,
I'm laughing, dear friend, thanks to you!

Green Dreams in Ceramic Pots

In pots of clay, the dreams do bloom,
Little soldiers in tidy rooms.
Green warriors reaching for the skies,
With ceramic shields and leafy ties.

They plot escapes while I'm asleep,
Silent conspiracies they keep.
Each dawn I find them in new poses,
Stubborn plants, who needs roses?

I told them stories of worlds afar,
And now they stare like they're my star.
With our laughter echoing through the day,
Their greens wear grins, come what may!

These silent pals with souls so bright,
Fill my heart with pure delight.
In ceramic pots, oh what a crew,
My green dreams dance, so fresh and new!

Nourished by the Warmth Within

In my cozy nook, they sway with glee,
Photosynthesis is their cup of tea.
They sip on sunlight, basking with flair,
Green giants whispering secrets in air.

I bring them snacks of water each week,
They smile at me, it feels so cheek.
But I think they'll grow arms and chatter loud,
If I keep spoiling them, I'll be so proud!

When the sun peeks through, it's a leafy rave,
A little party that they crave.
They shimmy and shake, their leaves a'flap,
I feel like I've entered some planty trap!

With every glance, they warm my heart,
Nourished by love, they play their part.
In this little world, we share our days,
With warmth and laughter, it's how we play!

Shades of Growth in Small Rooms

In tiny spaces, oh what a sight,
Different shades of green igniting bright.
With leafy tales and stories to share,
These little plants take up no air!

They stretch and yawn as I sip my tea,
They giggle softly, just them and me.
When I trip over pots, they cheer me on,
"In this jungle, you'll never be gone!"

Whispers of growth in cramped little beds,
Their leafy laughter fills up my head.
I stumble through routines, they sway with grace,
Dancing delight in our small little space!

So here's to growth where space is tight,
With cheeky greens that bring pure delight.
In shades of laughter, they bloom and thrive,
Small rooms grow big when we're so alive!

Breath of Life in Quiet Nooks

In a corner where sunlight beams,
Leaves stand tall, plotting green schemes.
Potted chums with secrets to share,
Whispering tales with leafy flair.

Laughter dances in the air,
As branches sway without a care.
The soil giggles, a bubbly friend,
Through roots and laughs, their joys extend.

A snail might race, if time could stop,
While shadows play hopscotch on the top.
Each sprout has dreams of growing wide,
In this nook where wittiness hides.

A gentle breeze brings jokes from afar,
As foliage sways to its own guitar.
With a tinge of humor in every leaf,
Nature's whispers turn doubt into belief.

Reflections of a Botanical Haven

In a room filled with green and delight,
Cacti gossip about the night.
With potted pals all in a row,
A silly show where leaves like to glow.

Reflections flirt upon the floor,
As spiders dance and drop down for more.
Basil teases the thyme with glee,
While mint rolls its eyes, crispy and free.

A plant stands proud, a real show-off,
While violets giggle, tossing a scoff.
Who knew a fern could crack such jokes,
In this haven where laughter evokes?

Light filters through, casting fun shades,
Where every sprout struts like parades.
With laughter sprouting from every pot,
This botanical tale can't be forgot.

Intricacies of Green Impressions

Leaves twirl around like dancers bright,
In the sun's glow, they swoon with delight.
A patch of moss takes a cozy nap,
While petals plot their own funny trap.

An ivy whispers with a cheeky grin,
"Hey, can you spare a twig for a spin?"
The soil chuckles, a laughter play,
As green friends sway in a whimsical way.

Tiny buds tickle the air's sweet breath,
Bringing giggles from their leafy depth.
Every shade wears a unique style,
As flowers bloom and pose for a while.

Sunshine winks through branches loose,
While nature perches in its juice.
With each green impression, humor unfurls,
Sprouting joy in this world of curls.

A Symphony of Leaves and Light

In a realm where leaves sing aloud,
A concert blooms under the crowd.
Photosynthesis beats on the roof,
As sunlight dances, a playful goof.

Branches strum with whispers sweet,
While worms wiggle to the blaring beat.
The sunbeam conductor waves so spry,
Conducting laughter from trees nearby.

Chlorophyll strings resonate on high,
While cardinals chirp in the sky.
Each sprout joins in, creating a rhyme,
A green melody transcending time.

The air is filled with botanical cheer,
As nature performs for all who hear.
In this symphony of leaves so bright,
Every moment's pure, laughing light.

Murmurs of the Living Room Forest

In the corner, she stands tall,
Leaves like fans, oh so enthralled.
Dust bunnies dance in her shade,
A jungle gym of green is made.

Whispers of growth in every leaf,
Telling tales of a shared belief.
Can they see me, sipping my tea?
Or laughing at my bad TV spree?

Couch cushions bear witness to my plight,
As I trip on roots in the night.
Who knew a plant could be so bold?
With a life story yet to be told!

Oh, to be that leafy queen,
In a world where I am a meme.
When the sunlight plays hide and seek,
That plant just smiles, so unique!

Nature’s Embrace in Indoor Spaces

A leafy figure in the room,
With style that chases away all gloom.
Knocking over my favorite mug,
But she doesn’t care; she's just a snug bug!

Petals whisper, “Life is a game,”
While I scold her, “Stop being lame!”
How could I scorn her green display?
When she brings life to my dull day!

A lumberjack hiding in plain view,
With roots that dance when the wind blows too.
She nods to the music that fills the air,
While I bust moves, without a care!

Oh, embrace me, leafy confidante,
Together we’ll dance, a lovely chant.
As laughter springs from my heart’s core,
Who knew home came with a leafy roar?

Silent Guardians of Sunlight

In the midst of the living room glow,
Stand silent sentinels, row by row.
Guardians of stories, they hold their ground,
In their leafy ambitions, joy is found.

They catch sunbeams, that's their game,
While I yell, "Stop playing lame!"
Each leaf a mirror, reflecting my blunders,
As I trip on a cat, oh the wonders!

With sparkling dust and a hint of sass,
The plants chuckle as I stumble past.
"Sorry, dear friend," I say with glee,
"Can't you see, it's just you and me?"

So here's to the friends with leafed-out charm,
Keeping me safe, raising alarms.
Together we make a wild array,
Gardening mishaps, come what may!

Verdant Tales in the Hearth's Glow

Brought indoors, she spins her tale,
A verdant saga of wind and gale.
Why does she roll her eyes at me?
Is that a wink, or just my spree?

We share secrets in the evening light,
Her leaves a chorus, my heart takes flight.
"Wait, what's that? A bug?" she cries,
And I jump up, with whirling eyes!

When the cat stalks with a hunting stare,
The plants chuckle; it's quite a pair.
"Hold your ground, you leafy crown!"
And I reel in laughter, what a showdown!

In this snug nook, all is well,
While nature thrives, I bid farewell.
With sparkles of humor in every frond,
We're a mismatched team, of which I'm so fond!

A Serenade to the Urban Oasis

In a pot that's green and round,
A plant with fronds, oh what a sound!
It sways and dances in the breeze,
Tickling me and all with ease.

I pour it water, sing a tune,
It groans and grins by afternoon,
It doesn't mind the city noise,
It plays the role of leafy joys.

I tell it jokes, it laughs along,
In this small space, we both belong.
It twirls around, a leafy chap,
We share our dreams, a leafy map.

With every leaf, my heart does swell,
This urban life, oh what a spell!
My leafy friend, so wise and bold,
Together we chase stories untold.

Glimmers in Leaf-Crowned Silence

In the hush of morning light,
A green giant's quite a sight.
It leans to hear the city hum,
In its world, it's never glum.

Oh, the tales it could disclose,
Of coffee spills and garden hose,
When neighbors pass with curious eyes,
It giggles softly, oh what a surprise!

With shiny leaves like emerald plates,
It greets the day as laughter waits.
Each raindrop falls a thoughtful gift,
To spark a dance, a joyful lift.

By dusk, it shrugs the sun away,
A leafy muse in funny play.
It tells the stars to light their way,
In leafy whispers, night's ballet.

Inner Worlds of Adventurous Fronds

Inside the pot, a wild affair,
My leafy mate is never bare.
It dreams of jungles, trees, and sun,
While I just hope to find some fun.

Each frond a tale, an outing planned,
To secret realms in leafy lands.
"Oh, take me to the place you roam!"
It sways and nods, I call it home.

We map the kitchen, every nook,
A jungle made with pots and books.
In every shadow, stories weave,
Adventure calls, we won't believe!

With every twist, the laughter grows,
In our small world, pure joy flows.
A leafy pal with daring style,
We wander far, with leaf-y smiles.

Murmurs of the Leafy Light

In the corner, where sunshine spills,
A leafy soul gives me the chills.
It watches as the world swirls by,
A plant so wise, it cannot lie.

"Is it too bright?" I often tease,
With leaves that dance like hidden keys.
It nods and sighs, with plenty flair,
This leafy life, we make a pair.

Between the cracks of urban dread,
We share our dreams, a yarn to thread.
It pokes its leaves, whispers so sweet,
There's comedy beneath green feet.

So here we sit, both laugh and sigh,
In our leafy world, we soar and fly.
Through every joke and sunny plight,
We flourish in this leafy light.

The Symphony of Photosynthesis

In the morning sun, they sway and dance,
Leaves twist in breezes, a leafy prance.
Photosynthesize like it's a breeze,
Sipping on sunshine with elegant ease.

Each petal laughs in the golden light,
Chlorophyll dreams make the colors bright.
Who knew the trees could throw a show?
Nature’s own band, putting on a glow!

Green to the left, a twirl to the right,
Leaves whisper secrets, oh what a sight!
Breezy banter with clouds up high,
Creating a symphony in the sky.

So grab your chairs, take a seat,
Join the green concert, can’t be beat!
A quirky tune for those who hear,
Nature’s orchestra, full of cheer!

Green Echoes in Still Air

In a garden quiet, secrets spill,
Echoes of green with time to kill.
Funny how petals wave hello,
To insects buzzing in quite a show!

Laughter erupts from the branches high,
A committee of leaves, oh me, oh my!
They gossip sweetly, in a rustle parade,
Every glance from them, a leafy trade.

Shadows dance gently on the ground,
As sunlight giggles, twirling around.
Leaves throw a party, a bash in the air,
Invite the bees; they're buzzing with flair!

In the stillness, humor unfolds,
With every breeze, a joke retold.
Nature's jesters, with laughs on display,
In green echoes where antics play!

Shadows of the Verdant Spirits

Amidst the green, shadows take flight,
Whispering stories in the soft light.
Spirits of nature, with giggles they glide,
Playing hide and seek, with leaves as their guide.

Branches croon with a tickling breeze,
Jokes of old trees as they bend their knees.
Roots chuckle softly beneath the clay,
While ladybugs join in the wild ballet.

Sunlight winks through a leafy screen,
Casting shadows, a playful scene.
Buds and blooms with cheeky grins,
In nature's game, everybody wins!

So dance with the shadows, full of cheer,
As trees become jesters, without fear.
In a green theater, laughter runs deep,
As spirits of verdant joys take a leap!

Leaves’ Language in Quiet Corners

In mute corners where whispers dwell,
Leaves have a language, can you tell?
They chatter in rustles, soft and light,
Sharing their secrets under the night.

Crisp edges flutter, a comic jest,
While branches giggle, they surely know best.
In the frosty air, a mischievous sigh,
Leaves are the jesters as time passes by.

In sunlit patches, they throw a ball,
Bouncing with laughter; oh what a haul!
The petals gossip, a riotous crew,
In the quiet corners, just me and you!

So listen closely, my friend, you’ll see,
The humor of nature’s whimsical spree.
In every leaf, a tale of delight,
In whispers of green, life feels so right!

Echoes of Nature in Glassy Rooms

In a room filled with light, oh what a sight,
Leaves dance like wild, all green and bright.
Photosynthesizing, they spin with glee,
Sipping on sunshine, how silly they be!

Reflections of green on polished floors,
Tropical dreams, behind closed doors.
Here comes a cat, with a leap and a pounce,
She thinks it’s a jungle, she'll take her chance!

Spilled some water, oh what a mess,
Slippery leaves in a joyous dress.
Plants chuckle softly, what a comical show,
Nature does love to put on a glow!

In the glassy rooms, laughter erupts,
As shadows of leaves play and disrupt.
With each little twitch, their antics are clear,
Nature's own jesters, bringing us cheer!

Curves of Serenity and Stillness

In corners they bend, so whimsically round,
Each leaf a dancer, to silence they're bound.
Breathe in their calm, with a hint of a grin,
These leafy companions, where laughter begins!

The wind through the cracks, brings whispers of cheer,
A leaf flutters down, 'Look, I'm flying, dear!'
Serenity laughs, while perched on a chair,
In this leafy haven, no worry to bear.

They stretch and they lean, in the sun's warm embrace,
As if sharing jokes, in a leafy race.
Curves of tranquility, waiting to spill,
With laughter of nature, we get our fill!

Stillness around them, yet life is so grand,
Nature's good humor, we all understand.
With every soft twist, their stories unfold,
In this calm wonderland, humor's pure gold!

The Art of Growing Together

Two plants sit side by side, quite a sight,
Gossiping leaves, in the warm evening light.
One says, 'Did you hear? The sun shines just right!'
The other responds, 'Yeah, but watch for the night.'

They twist and they tangle, roots all entwined,
Sharing their secrets, so wonderfully blind.
'What’s your secret to keeping so spry?'
'Well, I just drink water and wink at the sky!'

Together they thrive, their spirits are high,
Through springtime and storms, they never ask why.
One's a bit bushy, while the other is tall,
In this leafy ballet, they both have a ball!

The art of connection, they often espouse,
Jokes and puns whispered around the house.
As they grow side by side in this earthly tether,
It’s laughter and friendship that makes them together!

Tapestry of Verdant Hues

A patchwork of green, each leaf finely stitched,
In a tapestry bright, nature's been bewitched.
Laughter erupts from the plants on the sill,
Tickling each other, it’s a riotous thrill!

Textures and colors, a joyful delight,
Blushing in sunlight, glowing so bright.
The fern tells a story, while the palm simply sways,
In this living gallery, fun never decays.

With plucky adventures of each little sprout,
A chorus of green, with laughter throughout.
Quirky little friends, in pots they abide,
Sharing their tales, with no need to hide.

In a riot of hues, their joy is complete,
Jumbled up laughter, oh, isn't it sweet?
With chirps and with chuckles, they sway without care,
In this tapestry woven, love fills the air!

The Silent Dramaturgy of Greenery

In the corner, the pot stands still,
Waiting for sunlight, an unspoken thrill.
Leaves whisper secrets to shadows near,
Plotting a drama, full of cheer.

A cactus rolls its eyes in disdain,
Bored by the drama of leafy reign.
Pot to pot, they plot a grand play,
With mischief and laughter, they brighten the day.

A fern swoops in, takes the lead role,
While succulents giggle, feeling quite whole.
The stage is set for a leafy parade,
Nature's little jesters, unafraid.

As gravity tugs, one leaf takes a dive,
A comedy scene—oh, how they thrive!
In the sun's embrace, they prance and sway,
The potting drama goes on in a fray.

Diaries of the Leafed Heart

A leaf once wrote in a diary grand,
Of sunlit dreams and a strange, leafy band.
It penned down stories of raindrop delight,
And how the wind waltzed in the night.

A buddy beside, a twig turned the page,
Impressed by the tales, it felt quite sage.
But oh, the plot thickened, as mornings passed,
When the sun appeared, both giggled at last.

Snails left notes, written in slime,
Joining their chatter, taking their time.
In the leaf journal, laughter took flight,
As they crafted stories to soften the night.

And so they reflected, gleeful and spry,
Sharing their laughter beneath the sky.
Who knew that a leaf could have such wit?
With tales of the garden, they made quite a hit!

Serene Portraits Beneath the Canopy

Under the canopy, portraits arise,
With leafy models striking goofy guise.
Beneath the branches, creatures sway,
Making art in their silly play.

A leaf poses, with a twist and a bend,
While the branches laugh, a playful trend.
With sunlight painting colors bright,
Artistry thrives in the radiant light.

A beetle takes a bow, proud as can be,
While a butterfly flutters, full of glee.
Nature's gallery, a comedic scene,
Transforming the ordinary into the keen.

Together they dance in the gentle breeze,
Making portraits of joy, never to cease.
Underneath the cover, in moments combined,
Humor and art become intertwined.

Echoing Worlds of Verdant Life

In the tall grass, a rumor did sprout,
Of a secret world, with giggles throughout.
The leaves shared tales of dancing light,
In echoes of life, both weird and bright.

A toad gave a croak, a comedic flair,
As daisies burst out, just to declare—
“We’re a forest of fun, where laughter's the key!
Join in the chorus, come sing with me!”

The bumblebees buzzed with a joyful hum,
While the ants marched by, all feeling the scrum.
Each step was a joke, each leaf a delight,
In the echoing world, everything felt right.

So let’s share these moments beneath the skies,
In this verdant life, where humor always flies.
For nature’s a jest, in its own playful way,
Creating our smiles in a charming display.

Tapestry of Verdant Dreams

In a pot so grand, a leaf does dance,
Waving to friends, it takes a chance.
Spinning tales of sunlight beams,
Whispering secrets of leafy dreams.

A twisty stem, it sways with flair,
Daring the cat to stop and stare.
In this green world, the jokes are lush,
Even the dust bunnies start to hush.

When watering's done, it splashes cheer,
Applauding itself for being here.
A growth spurt hit, it’s earned a crown,
The plant king laughs as the sun goes down.

So raise a glass to this leafy chap,
A botanical buddy, full of sap.
In this tapestry green and bold,
Every leaf's a story waiting to be told.

The Art of Leaf and Light

Dancing leaves catch the morning glow,
In the living room, they steal the show.
A curious drape, they twist and tease,
Tickling the air with a gentle breeze.

Light filters down on their vibrant hue,
Turns ordinary moments into something new.
They strike a pose, oh what a sight!
Who knew green friends could bring such delight?

Whispering greenery in a jolly spree,
Inviting everyone for tea with glee.
"Are you thirsty?" they mischievously ask,
As they sip from the light, a leafy flask.

Each leaf a brushstroke in this lively art,
Creating a canvas, a true work of heart.
So here's to nature's quirky play,
In the gallery of life, they lead the way.

Beneath the Botanical Glow

Underneath the glow of a soft lamp light,
Leaves gather round, ready for a fright.
"Did you hear?" one leaf starts to crack,
"Someone's got a new pot, let's make a pact!"

With every twist, giggles fill the air,
Leaves curl up, showing they care.
"Don't lose your touch; keep your shade tight!"
They chuckle and shimmer into the night.

A household of greens, united and spry,
They plot pranks with the help of nearby sky.
With stories to share and sunlight to chase,
Their indoor jungle is a lively place.

So here's to the greens that play and grow,
Under the glow, they steal the show.
With every burst of joy and sweet song,
The dance of leaves carries all along.

Secrets of the Indoor Jungle

In the heart of the home, a jungle thrives,
Where curious leaves pretend to be spies.
Peeking through windows, they plot and plan,
To catch the squirrel, their biggest fan.

At dinner, they eavesdrop on every chat,
"Did you hear how the dog chewed the mat?"
They laugh in green, with humor so sly,
Creating legends that float through the sky.

Somersaults sprouted in the afternoon light,
A leafy parade, a comical sight.
"Watch us prance!" the verdant ones shout,
"The indoors is ours, without a doubt!"

So cherish the plants, the quirky green crew,
With their glee and laughter, they brighten the view.
In this secret world where laughter rings,
The joys of the jungle are wonderful things.

Views from a Pot

In my little pot, I sit so proud,
With leaves like umbrellas, I quite draw a crowd.
The sun shines bright, but oh what a fuss,
When I sway to the left, there's a fuss from the bus!

Bugs drop by for tea, uninvited though,
They sip my sap like it's a trendy show.
I roll my eyes and say, 'Not today!'
These pests need a guidebook, they've lost their way!

Every droplet that falls, I treat like a show,
As if it's a curtain, and voilà, let it flow!
Giant leaves catch whispers of winds on the street,
Dance for the squirrels, now that's quite a feat!

Oh, views from my pot, such comedic delight,
Nature's own sitcom, from morn until night.
I chuckle and wiggle, with roots firmly set,
In this leafy cabaret, I'm quite the vignette!

The Pulse of Indoor Eden

In the corner it sits, my leafy delight,
With a wink of a leaf, it's a real featherweight.
Tickling the curtains in a jovial jest,
While plotting its next leafy party fest!

Photosynthesis groove, oh what a cha-cha,
Making food from sunlight, like a leafy star!
With my cozy plant rule, I cheerfully chime,
Who knew being green could be such a crime?

Plants gossip of pollen, like tea-spillers bold,
Each telling tall tales, leaf stories unfold.
I chuckle in silence, just watering my brood,
Living in this Eden, who can't help but brood?

With a quirky arrangement, what has begun,
In this green-filled chaos, we laugh and we run.
So here's to the fun, the joys and the winks,
In our pulse of chaos, we're friends and we think!

Reflections in the Morning Dew

In the dawn's early light, I see glimmers of fun,
Dew drops like diamonds, scattered and spun.
My leaves are in jest, stretching wide for a show,
Winking at sunlight, 'Oh, come on—let's glow!'

Rabbits hop by, taking care not to stare,
While I have a chat with a breeze through the air.
Leafy voices giggling, it's a delightful dance,
Where nature and laughter go hand in hand—what a chance!

Each droplet reflects, like laughter in grace,
Mirrored mischief playing on every green face.
They say I'm just foliage, but I know the score,
With every drop glistening, I humorously soar!

The morning hangs breezy, the world's still at ease,
Here in my garden, laughter drapes like a tease.
So roll on, sweet sun, let the fun dew drop,
For in this verdant world, the giggles won't stop!

Whirling Dervishes of Foliage

In whirlwinds of green, we twirl and we sway,
Dancing like dervishes, come join in the play!
Leaves twisted and turned, with laughter in chorus,
Who knew a plant could incite such euphoria?

Round and round we go, a leafy ballet,
While sunbeams tickle, teasing us all day.
When the wind picks up, oh, what a surprise!
We shimmy and shake under generous skies!

Petals gleam brightly, like stars in the night,
While roots dig deep, finding courage and light.
We're not just green things, we have style and flair,
Mimicking dances, unbothered and rare!

So come join our party, out here in the sun,
Where leaves laugh with joy, and everyone's won.
In this crazy garden, with laughter replete,
Whirling dervishes, we move to our beat!

The Lullaby of Indoor Greenery

In the corner of the room, it sways with grace,
Whispering secrets in its leafy embrace.
A plant with dreams, growing taller each day,
It dances to the music of sunlight's play.

When dust bunnies gather, it gives a soft sigh,
"Just one more leaf," it tells the passing fly.
Its roots are a party, underground they play,
Sipping on water, while making a mess all day.

At night, it plots, oh the tales that it weaves,
Of mossy adventures and mischievous thieves.
With twirls and twiddles, it shows off its style,
In the heart of the home, making everyone smile.

So here's to the greenery that brings us a cheer,
With laughter and joy, it draws everyone near.
Let's toast to the jokes that this plant loves to tell,
In the lullaby world where indoor greens dwell.

Tangles of Growth and Dream

A plant in a pot wears a crown of delight,
With leaves in a tangle, what a curious sight!
It stretches and yawns, as if waking from dreams,
Daring to grow in the sun's golden beams.

It whispers to shadows, "Let's dance in the light!"
Gather round pals, it's a botanical fight.
With vines laced in giggles, they twist and they sway,
In a room full of laughter, they brighten the day.

When the cat makes a leap, the leaves play it cool,
"I'm just a tall snack, don't be such a fool."
But the feline just ponders, "How can this be?
A plant with a sense of humor, oh me!"

As night falls, it dreams of a world full of fun,
Of radishes racing and peas on the run.
Amid tangled ambitions, this plant finds its groove,
Growing wild with laughter, in a dance that will soothe.

The Tuning Fork of the Leaves

In a pot by the window, it catches the rays,
Reaching for music in whimsical ways.
With a rustle and whisper, it starts to hum,
A melody bounces, the fiddlehead strums.

Each leaf is a note, a burst of green sound,
Strumming the air, spreading joy all around.
When friends come to visit, it plays a new song,
“Join in with your laughter, you can't go wrong!”

The soil is a stage, and the roots tap their feet,
In rhythm with life, in the pulse of the heat.
Its branches throw parties, for bugs on a spree,
“Don't be shy, little critters, come join the glee!”

As the evening draws close and the stars start to shine,
The plant strikes a chord; it’s a night full of wine.
With a giggle and wiggle, it nods to the moon,
In the symphony’s center, where laughter will bloom.

Inward Journeys of Verdant Souls

In a world of green, they plot and confer,
With whispers of wisdom, oh how they deter!
What if we flourish, and dance on the sill?
Inward journeys commence, oh what a thrill!

The sunlight's a friend, with warmth in its glow,
Encouraging growth, as they gently grow.
With roots like reporters, they gather their tales,
"More leaves for the gossip!" their laughter prevails.

When dust mites descend, they roll up in cheer,
"We thrive in this chaos, there's nothing to fear!"
Caterpillars too, come for a chat and a snack,
In the gardens of laughter, there's never a lack.

So raise up a glass to the souls of the green,
With journeys so funny, they make the world keen.
In the heart of our homes, their stories take flight,
With chuckles and giggles, they live in delight.

Leaves' Soliloquy in Sunbeam

Under the sun, they dance and sway,
Telling tales in the light of day.
"Hey there, you, what's the gossip here?"
They giggle, grown-up trees, full of cheer.

Breezes tickle, they start to tease,
"Look at us, we're the best of leaves!"
They rustle with joy, a leafy brigade,
Making fun of roots, a playful charade.

Caterpillars plot while they munch,
"We'll be butterflies, go on, take a punch!"
The leaves just roll with laughter and glee,
"Good luck, my friend, that's your next cup of tea."

With a flourish, they flash their green hues,
"Join our club, we share all the news!"
In the dappled sun, they shine so bright,
Frolicking leaves, in pure delight.

Veiled in Green: A Whisper's Tale

A canopy of green, secrets unfold,
Whispers of mischief, daring and bold.
"Did you see that bird?" a new leaf exclaims,
"He thinks he's a star! Oh, the shame, the shame!"

Laughter rings out from the uppermost tier,
"We told him, don't sing! He can't bring out cheer!"
Their gossip cascades like raindrops of fun,
As shadows play hide-and-seek in the sun.

A breeze floats by, and they start to sway,
"What is that smell? Is it lunch or a play?"
Even the ants start to tap in delight,
For a picnic beneath their foliage bright.

"Shh! Don't scare the squirrels! They're rehearsing a show,"
Pointing at acorns all lined in a row.
"If they drop the script, it's a total faux pas!"
In laughter, the leaves carry on from afar.

Terra's Dreams in Urban Spaces

In the cityscape, they dream out loud,
"Hey, look at us, we're a leafy crowd!"
Concrete giants tower, but we stay spry,
Roots in the cracks, oh how we fly!

Pigeons stroll by, with a swaggering flair,
"What's the latest? We're too cool to care!"
"Just soaking up sun, living our best,
And plotting to outshine, just like the rest!"

Traffic hums loudly, but we're in a trance,
"Cut through the noise, let our leaves take a dance!"
As window boxes burst with colors so bright,
Streetlights twinkle, offering their light.

A whimsical breeze lifts their spirits high,
"Join us, dear world, let's all dance and fly!"
For in urban spaces, these whispers unite,
Creating a canvas, a beautiful sight.

Nestled in Shades of Nature

In the forest's embrace, they lounge with ease,
Whispering jokes to the buzzing bees.
"Did you hear the one 'bout the curious seed?"
"He wanted to sprout, but forgot how to lead!"

The woods are their stage, and they take a bow,
"We're nature's stand-up, just ask the cow!"
Ferns flicker their fronds and giggle with glee,
"What a silly world, come join our spree!"

The stream joins in with a bubbly laugh,
"We're all part of this nature's path!"
Rabbits hop and the deer lean in closer,
For a comedy show, nature's a composer.

"So gather around, let's make shadows dance,
For life is a jest, come on, take a chance!"
In this shade of delight, where all laugh as one,
They bask in green glory, enjoying the fun.

www.ingramcontent.com/pod-product-compliance
Lightning Source LLC
Chambersburg PA
CBHW070331120526
44590CB00017B/2851
9781805812968